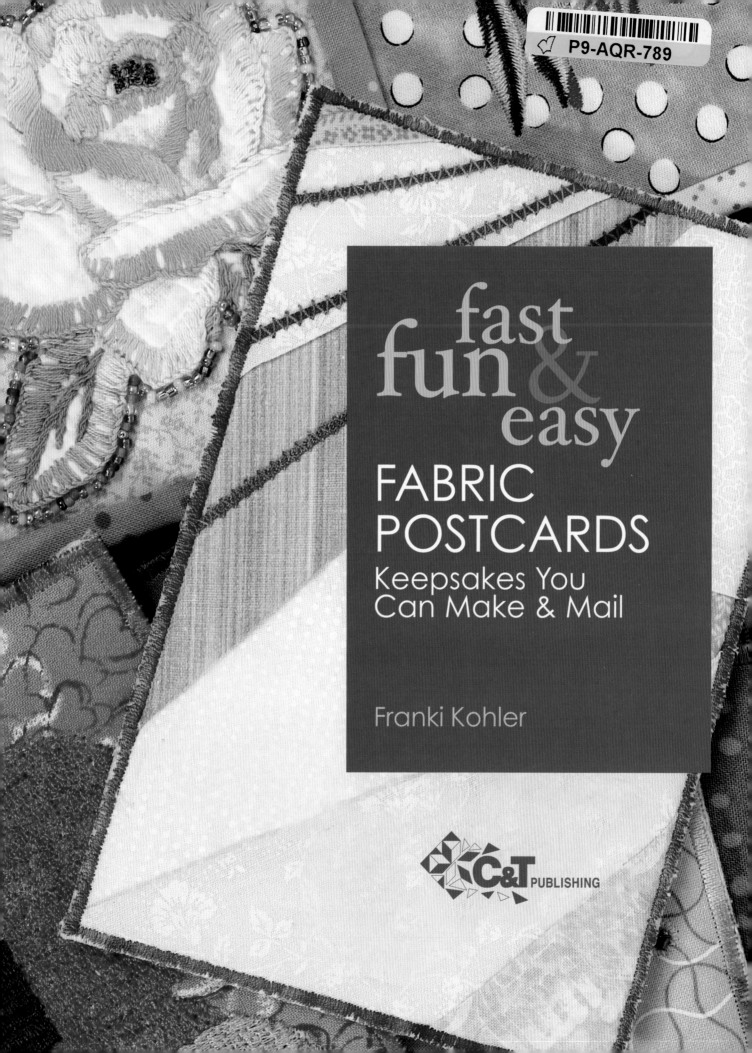

fast fun & easy
FABRIC POSTCARDS
Keepsakes You Can Make & Mail

Franki Kohler

C&T PUBLISHING

C&T Publishing

Text © 2006 Franki Kohler

Artwork © 2006 C&T Publishing

Publisher: Amy Marson

Editorial Director: Gailen Runge

Acquisitions Editor: Jan Grigsby

Editor: Liz Aneloski

Technical Editors: Gailen Runge, Teresa Stroin

Copyeditor/Proofreader: Wordfirm Inc.

Design Director/Cover & Book Designer: Kristy K. Zacharias

Illustrator: Tim Manibusan

Production Assistant: Zinnia Heinzmann

Photography: Diane Pedersen and Luke Mulks (unless otherwise noted)

Published by C&T Publishing, Inc., P.O. Box 1456, Lafayette, CA 94549

Library of Congress Cataloging-in-Publication Data

Kohler, Franki.

  Fast, fun & easy fabric postcards : keepsakes you can make & mail / Franki Kohler.

    p. cm.

  Includes bibliographical references.

  ISBN-13: 978-1-57120-332-8 (paper trade)

  ISBN-10: 1-57120-332-X (paper trade)

  1. Machine sewing. 2. Textile crafts. 3. Postcards. I. Title: Fast, fun and easy fabric postcards. II. Title.

  TT713.K655 2006

  746–dc22

  2005029854

Printed in China

10 9 8 7 6 5 4 3 2 1

Dedication

In memory of my grandmother Hilda Elizabeth Packer Preston, who gave me an appreciation for work with needle and thread and whose mantra was, "If it's worth doing, it's worth doing well." I miss you still.

Acknowledgments

Special awards should go to:

My husband, David, who always responds with, "That's great! You'll do a good job with [fill in the blank]. Let me know how I can help." No matter what I've taken on!

My sister and quilting buddy, Christy Cutting, who is always supportive and inspirational.

My friend, Susan Terry, who loaned me the *Quilting Arts Magazine* that started this journey, and for her comments and suggestions—always worth seeking out. We're flyin' now!

Gael Betts, Sally Morris, and Dale Robards for their enthusiasm and valued insights.

All the wonderful artists of art2mail and Postmark'd Art who so graciously share their skills and knowledge and are a never-ending source of inspiration. I'm so proud to be a part of both of these groups, and I treasure every postcard I receive. Extra heaps of gratitude go to the artists who allowed me to use their fabric postcards as examples: Sharon Benton, Kathie Briggs, Jenni Paige, Darma Redwine, Janice Simpson, Ellen Slattery, Margarete Steinhauer, Debra Svedberg, and Laurie Walton.

The talented and daring team at C&T, who decided to take a chance on me: Amy Marson, Gailen Runge, Jan Grigsby, Liz Aneloski, Sara Kate MacFarland, Diane Pedersen, and Luke Mulks—thank you.

Contents

Gramma Would Be Proud

introduction: art in the mail

My mail carrier approaches. My ears perk up. I rush to the mailbox. Receiving a fabric postcard in the mail is a real thrill for me.

My postcard adventures began when a friend handed me the summer 2004 issue of *Quilting Arts Magazine.* That issue contained an article about a group of artists who were making and exchanging fabric postcards. This was my "Eureka!" moment. With so many new techniques and products on the quilting market, I had been searching for a small format for experimentation, a format that required a minimum of time and material investment to teach me the new skills I wanted to learn.

I couldn't get to my computer fast enough to learn more, and the first thing I learned was that participating in a fabric postcard exchange was open to me. I joined Postmark'd Art and, later, art2mail. Now I could not only learn by making postcards, I could also learn by receiving them and seeing the work of other artists.

But you don't have to join a group to make and share these miniature treasures. Just review the special occasions you celebrated with friends and family in the past year—these are all occasions to make a fabric postcard. You learn new techniques; they get something special in the mail.

The most frequently asked question about mailing fabric postcards is, "Will the post office *really* deliver these?" The answer is "Yes!" The postcards should measure 4 inches by 6 inches and be no more than ⅛ inch thick; be decorated with small, flat embellishments (sequins, ink, stitches, small seed and bugle beads) so they won't be damaged in handling; and be able to carry postage. Postcards that meet these standards can be mailed to any U.S. address for the first-class postage rate. Choose a self-adhesive stamp—preferably one that coordinates with the design—and press it firmly in place. It's that easy!

If your postcard falls outside the standards set by the Postal Service, you can expect to be charged additional postage, but it can *still* be mailed. Postcards destined outside the United States will require additional postage, of course, but will be delivered without a problem. In addition to U.S. artists, I have traded fabric postcards with artists in Canada, Scotland, Taiwan, New Zealand, and Australia.

Still skeptical about being able to mail a fabric postcard? Then do what I did: Make one today and mail it to yourself. Make notes on the message side of the card to record the materials you used, or simply jot down a favorite inspirational quote. Don't forget to give your art a title, and date and sign the postcard for future reference. Then watch for your mail carrier!

I have chosen six projects to teach you the basics. Adjust them to suit your own taste and sense of design. I think making postcards is like nibbling a favorite finger treat; once you start, it's hard to stop!

the basics

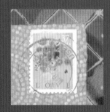

This chapter outlines the materials, tools, and techniques you'll need for making the fabric postcard projects that follow. Read through this chapter, and then challenge yourself to try something new with each card you make. Refer back here when you need a bit of clarification.

Basic Supplies

fabrics

Five of the projects in this book use 100% cotton fabric, and one project uses polyester organza over 100% cotton. Because you don't need to be concerned about washing the postcard, you are free to use any type of fabric that meets your design needs. This opens your option to decorator fabrics, printed fabrics used for sheeting, napkins, bandanas—you get the idea. A touch of lamé, organza, or other delicate fabrics might be just the thing you need to complete a design. Don't shy away from delicate fabrics; just have your pressing cloth handy to protect them from the heat of the iron.

Don't overlook the possibility of using treasured textile fragments. I have a small collection of items my grandmother decorated using many of her skills—Broderie Perse, embroidery, crochet, and tatting, to name a few. The textile she decorated might be in poor condition, but the individual designs are well worth the trouble to recycle (see *Gramma Would Be Proud* on page 3 and *Grandmother's Roses* on page 28).

stabilizer

Even a small appliqué or minimal decorative stitching will need a stabilizer to ensure that your fabric remains smooth and your stitches don't pucker. My favorite product is Pellon Shirtailor fusible nonwoven interfacing. Follow the manufacturer's directions for fusing Shirtailor to the wrong side of your fabric. Leave the stabilizer in place when you have finished stitching. It will stabilize beads, sequins, or other small embellishments you choose to stitch to the design.

If you choose a stabilizer that does not have fusible web on it, you will need a piece of paper-backed fusible web to fuse the stabilizer to your design fabric.

the filling

The fabric postcard has three layers, just like a quilt. It has a design side, an address and message side, and some kind of filling in between. Your choice of filling will determine how the card feels and the postcard's success in reaching its destination intact. All three fillings discussed below can be machine and/or hand stitched. I use both fast2fuse and Timtex with equal success and prefer them over the softer, more flexible feel of batting. I used fast2fuse for all of the projects in this book.

fast2fuse

fast2fuse is a stiff interfacing with fusible web on both sides; it is made of 75% polyester and 25% rayon. It arrives at your local quilt shop on a bolt (10 yards, 28 inches wide), so you can purchase it by the yard. It is manufactured in two thicknesses. Choose the thinner version (less than 1/8 inch thick) for the postcards. It is lightweight and can be fused using a steam iron. I enjoy the convenience of having the fusible web already on this product.

easy!

Cut 5″ strips of fast2fuse. Each strip will yield 4 rectangles 5″ × 7″.

Timtex

Timtex is a 1/8″-thick stiff interfacing made of 70% polyester and 30% rayon. It can be purchased by mail order in a 13 1/2″ × 22″ package (see page 47) or by the yard from a bolt (10 yards, 22″ wide) at your local fabric store. It is lightweight and can be steam ironed. This product does not have fusible web on it.

Batting

If you want a softer look and feel for the postcard, use one or two layers of thin cotton batting, such as Quilters Dream Cotton or Warm and Natural. You will also need two or three pieces of paper-backed fusible web—one piece for between each layer of batting (to hold your layers together), one to fuse the front, and one to fuse the back. You will need to experiment with batting to find the number of layers most pleasing to you. Keep in mind that if your post-card is too thick for postal regulations, you will be required to pay additional postage for mailing it.

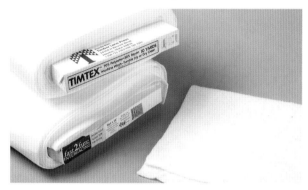

fast2fuse, Timtex, cotton batting

paper-backed fusible web

Fusible web holds the three layers of your postcard together. It also adds a bit more body. I have used several products, and I prefer Pellon Wonder-Under. Choose a lightweight to medium-weight fusible that has a paper backing that peels off easily. Avoid heavyweight products; the extra adhesive will end up on your needle and make stitching difficult.

fast!

Precut fusible web and fast2fuse or Timtex. Place each in a resealable plastic bag and put them in a basket near your iron. They are ready to use at home or can be packed quickly if you need to take them somewhere.

thread

There is only one rule for thread. If it enhances your design, use it! Cotton, rayon, polyester, nylon, perle cotton, metallic, glow-in-the-dark: Each will be useful in a different way, depending on your design.

One word of caution: While nylon thread does that wonderful job of seeming to disappear into the fabric, it also has a good chance of melting when you fuse the design to the postcard filling. I use MonoPoly, by Superior Threads. It is made of poly-ester, comes in .004 size on a 2,400-yard spool, is soft and pliable, will not discolor, and has a high heat resistance. You may find it useful for many other sewing needs as well.

fast!

Avoid the mishap of grabbing the wrong thread for a project. Store spools and bobbins of nylon, Mono-Poly, and glow-in-the-dark threads in individual, clearly marked plastic bags.

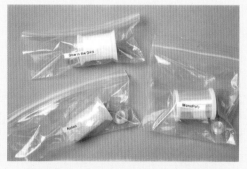

MonoPoly, nylon, glow-in-the-dark threads

Don't overlook thread weight as a possible design feature. A lightweight thread can blend easily, pro-vide a small shadow effect, or seem to disappear altogether. A heavyweight thread can fill in an area quickly and provide bulk and dimension to the design. See more on this subject in *Let the Stitches Speak* (see pages 23–27).

Bobbin Thread

Most of my stitching for the design side of the postcard is done using a white polyester specialty bobbin thread. Because I stitch on the design side of the postcard before the project is layered, the bobbin thread doesn't show. I find that using this type of thread means I have less lint buildup in the bobbin case area. The bobbin will hold a lot of this lightweight thread, so you will spend your time sewing, not refilling bobbins. Bobbin thread is available in white and colors, on spools, cones, and prewound bobbins.

Bobbin thread

Coordinate the bobbin thread with the fabric when you do bobbin thread work or when the bobbin thread will be seen. The latter is true when the edge of the postcard is stitched with a satin or decorative stitch (see Getting on the Edge on pages 18–19).

Nymo Beading Thread

This nylon thread is available in several thicknesses and colors. I use size D and keep white, gray, and black handy. This size is strong enough to secure beads and other small embellishments to your design and thin enough to pass through a small seed bead twice.

Nymo beading thread

easy!

When you finish stitching and are replacing the thread, hold the thread at the needle with your left hand, snip the thread free at your fabric, and then at the top of the machine. Pull the thread from the needle down through the machine. This "flossing" will help keep your machine clear of thread snags.

Hold thread at needle and snip.

Snip at the top and pull down through the machine.

fun!

Tape a small bag near your sewing machine. Toss your "flossing" threads into it. Use the threads to create your own fun design (see *Time Travel* under Variations on page 27).

Basic Tools

You will need the following tools:

- ☐ rotary cutter: Use one with a safety feature.
- ☐ mat: Your large cutting mat will work, but you might like using a smaller mat for the postcards.
- ☐ 6″ × 12″ ruler

- scissors: Small pointed scissors and curved embroidery scissors
- viewfinder: Cut a 4″ × 6″ opening in the middle of a 5½″ × 8½″ piece of black card stock. One 8½″ × 11″ sheet will yield 2 viewfinders.

Cutting tools and viewfinder

easy!

When creating the design for your postcard, you will make it larger than needed (5″ × 7″ instead of 4″ × 6″). Use the viewfinder to select the area of the design you will use.

ironing supplies

A firm ironing surface works best for fusing the postcard sandwich together. If you have a small, portable ironing board, use it.

You will need a protective covering for your ironing board when you are fusing stabilizer or fusible web to fabric. My favorite for this protection is a Teflon sheet (see Sources on page 47). Absolutely nothing will adhere to it, so any gunk that gets on it is easily wiped off with a soft rag. It will last for years. Parchment paper is an alternative.

You will want a pressing cloth handy to protect any metallic or other heat-sensitive threads or embellishments.

No matter how fastidious you are, you will probably end up with fusible adhesive on your iron. Be prepared, so you can grab the hot-iron cleaner and take care of it right away.

Ironing supplies

marking tools

Use your preferred marking tool to mark the 4-inch by 6-inch area on your design fabric. This mark is the cutting line, so color or permanence of the line is not an issue. Use a permanent-ink pen for hand-writing or drawing on fabric for the design or address side of the postcard.

sewing machine

Your sewing machine should be capable of sewing a zigzag stitch in several widths. Refer to your instruction manual, and become comfortable adjusting tension for top and bobbin thread. This skill will allow you to more fully use the machine's capabilities. The capabilities of your machine will determine which techniques you can use to create your postcards. A machine with decorative stitches is required for *Let the Stitches Speak* (see page 23).

Presser Feet

An even-feed foot will allow you to stitch through several layers of fabric without fear of unwanted tucks or bunching. I use this foot to sew decorative stitches. Use a darning foot for free-motion stitching and an appliqué foot for machine appliqué and finishing the edge of the postcard (see Getting on the Edge on pages 18–19).

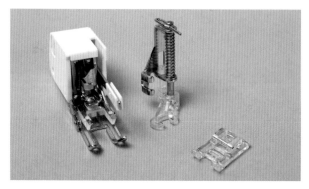

Even-feed foot, darning foot, and appliqué foot

easy!

Be kind to your machine and reduce emergency repair trips midproject by maintaining your sewing machine according to the manufacturer's instructions for cleaning and oiling.

Bobbin Case

Your sewing machine bobbin case came with a tension setting determined by the factory. This setting will be good for most of your general sewing needs. As you experiment with sewing techniques and varieties of threads, however, you will find it useful to have a second bobbin case. Adjust your bobbin tension by turning the small screw on the side of the case. Think of the screw as the face of a clock. If the slot is set at 11 o'clock, turn to 10 o'clock to loosen, 12 o'clock to tighten. Always make adjustments by one hour at a time and test the setting.

Tension screw

Bobbin case

fast!

Invest in an extra bobbin case. Mark it with red nail polish so you won't confuse the one you adjust with the one you leave at the factory setting.

fun!

Keep a test scrap by every sewing machine you own. Mine has three layers: one light fabric, one layer thin batting, one dark fabric. It's easy to check for machine tension or thread color compatibility with this simple tool.

Test tension and thread choices here, not on your project.

Computerized Embroidery Machine

Most major sewing machine manufacturers offer models that have built-in computerized embroidery software. In addition to the designs featured in this software, many more designs are available on programmed cards, disks, CDs, and by downloading through a vendor on the Internet. You can also purchase software that will enable you to create (digitize) your own designs. I've had Starbird, Inc., digitize designs for me (see Sources on page 47). To digitize your images, contact Starbird or search the Internet for other companies that offer this service.

If you don't own an embroidery machine, don't skip the chapter on embroidery. Read through it—you might find inspiration or options that are useful.

easy!

If you have a computerized sewing machine, take care to have your machine plugged into a surge protector at all times. This piece of equipment will protect your computer from damage caused by a surge, spike, or other harmful electrical imbalance.

decorative stitches

The symbol the manufacturer has chosen to represent a particular stitch on your machine isn't always an accurate representation of how it will look when it is stitched on fabric. The only way you will truly know what stitches you have is by sewing each built-in stitch on fabric. This is a good way to have a visual catalog of stitches available for quick review.

Fuse Pellon Shirtailor fusible nonwoven interfacing or freezer paper to the wrong side of a solid-colored fabric. Trim to 8½″ × 11″. Use a pencil to draw a line down the center of the width of the fabric page. Thread the machine with a contrasting thread. Select a stitch and sew to the drawn line. Select the next stitch and sew to the end of the fabric. Continue selecting stitches and sewing until you have sewn a sample of all the stitches on your machine. Use a Pigma pen to write the number of the stitch under the line of decorative stitching. Tuck into a clear plastic page sleeve and keep in a binder with other information on your machine.

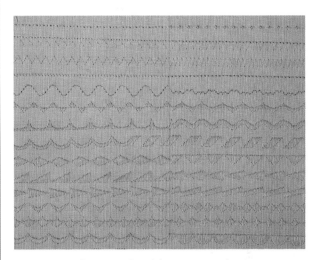

Sewn samples of decorative stitches

The exercises in *Let the Stitches Speak* (see pages 24–26) are a good starting point for experimenting with your stitches.

needles

Start every new project (or every eight hours of sewing) with a new needle in your sewing machine. Experiment to find the needles that work best for the types of threads you use, and keep plenty of each type on hand. Here are the needles I use:

- topstitch 80/20 or Microtex sharp for 40- to 50-weight rayon thread

- topstitch 90/14 or Jeans for Jeans Stitch thread, 12-weight cotton or Superior Glitter

- titanium 75/11 for multiple layers of fusible or Sulky Sticky

- twin 2.0/80, 3.0/75, 4.0/80, 4.0/90 for stitching one design with two colors of thread at the same time

- metallica or topstitch 80/12, 90/14 for metallic thread

- embroidery or 75/11 for 40- to 50-weight thread for embroidery design

- shadow work twin embroidery for stitching one embroidery design with two colors of thread to create a shadow effect

Basic Techniques

The projects for this book were chosen to demonstrate just a few of the possibilities for design creation and to get you to dabble in a variety of techniques. Once you've made a card or two, the ideas for new ones will crowd your brain!

preparation for printing on fabric

The possibilities for using photographs, clip art, maps, and text as design elements on postcards are unlimited. Printing a message and the address of the recipient on the card is also a snap. If you have a computer and printer, you have the technology. With a scanner you can use vintage photographs without worrying about damaging them. There are two key ingredients to successful printing on fabric: fabric preparation and stabilizer.

Fabric Preparation

I prefer to prepare my own fabric for printing rather than using a heat-set transfer sheet. The process is easy and very economical. Bubble Jet Set 2000 comes in a 32 oz. bottle and prepares 100% cotton and 100% silk fabrics to be printed on with an ink-jet or bubble-jet printer. Follow the simple instructions on the product, and your printed image will be permanent and washable. Without pretreating your fabric, the slightest moisture will cause the ink to run, ruining your image. Bubble Jet Rinse comes in a 16 oz. bottle and is specifically designed to remove the Bubble Jet Set 2000 and excess ink from the printing process (it can cause some fading, depending on your printer and settings). It contains no perfumes or bleach. Follow the instructions on the product for best results (see Sources on page 47).

Stabilizer

For success *every* time, I use Pellon Wonder-Under paper-backed fusible web. Not only does the fusible web stabilize the fabric so it will glide through the printer easily, but the image is now ready to cut out and become part of the design (photograph) or fuse to the postcard filling for the message/address side (written document). Freezer paper is an alternative, but be sure the paper and fabric have completely bonded, or the edges might get caught in the printer.

Printing Steps

Printing on these smaller pieces of fabric works best if you treat them like envelopes. Use the envelope-feed slot if your printer has one (follow the directions below), or make the paper feed adjustments recommended in your printer manual.

1. Fuse paper-backed fusible web to white fabric (for a photograph) or coordinated fabric (for the address side). Trim to 4″ × 6½″.

2. Select the image (or written document) and prepare it for printing.

3. Select printer paper size 4″ × 6″.

4. Select "envelope manual feed."

5. Place stabilized fabric, paper side up, in the envelope-feed slot of the printer.

6. Print the image (or document).

collage

The fun of collage design is in the hunt for the objects. Some of the most mundane objects can create a striking image (see *Labels* and *Care Instructions* under Variations on page 34, for instance). And who wouldn't smile at receiving the gift of time as with *Time in a Bottle* (see Variations on page 34)? The bottom line? Anything flat works.

Using Beads

Use beads with abandon; just keep two things in mind: They might be put through a post office machine, even if you ask for hand cancellation. The beads need an extra stitch to secure them in place. It's hard for me *not* to add a bead or two to every postcard I make. I regularly use size 11° seed beads (Japan and Czech Republic), size 11° Delica (Japan), or size 11° Tri Bead. I also use size 2° and 3° bugle beads and twisted bugles without a hitch.

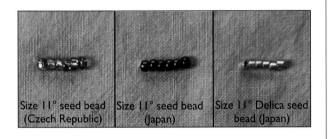

| Size 11° seed bead (Czech Republic) | Size 11° seed bead (Japan) | Size 11° Delica seed bead (Japan) |

Size 11° Tri Bead, 2° and 3° bugle beads, twisted bugles

Using Scrapbooking Supplies

Your local craft and scrapbooking stores have an incredible variety of ready-to-use embellishments to personalize your postcards. Items on paper, vellum, ribbon, fabric, and metal are all possibilities as long as they are flat enough and have some way of being attached.

Ready-to-use embellishments

Using Yarn

You don't have to be a knitter to appreciate the beautiful yarn available today. *Santa Baby, Hurry Down the Chimney Tonight!* (see Variations on page 39) uses it for the fringe on Santa's cap, and *Flowers Brighten the Bluest Day* (see Variations on page 42) uses yarn to enhance the background. Another version of *Flowers Brighten the Bluest Day* (see Getting on the Edge (D) on page 19) uses yarn under the netting to create the background *and* includes yarn stitched to the edge.

Using Tulle, Netting, and Organza

These three fabrics are so useful for design and attaching embellishments that I wouldn't be without them. Tulle is handy for capturing a design element so the edges won't get caught in handling (see *Kimono Ladies and Fans* under Variations on page 34, *Time Travel* and *Spring Greens* under Variations on page 27, and *Counterpoint* under Variations on page 46). I keep tulle handy in colors ranging from very light to black. Tulle does double duty on *Time in a Bottle* (see Variations on page 34):

It captures the watch findings and creates the shape of the bottle. Netting was used to capture yarn on *Flowers Brighten the Bluest Day* (see Variations on page 42). Dotted organza and tulle were used to create *Sun Spots* (see Have You Met Angelina? on page 43).

Tulle, netting, organza

Paper Piecing

This is a fun way to use the fabric scraps you have saved from other projects, while creating a more interesting background for a design. Use the paper-piecing pattern on page 33.

When paper piecing, use a small stitch length (#1.5–1.8, or 18–20 stitches per inch) and sew and pin on the side of the paper with the lines. The fabric pieces do not need to be perfect shapes, and you don't have to worry about the grain of the fabric. But it's a *very* good idea to use a scrap that is at least ¾˝ larger all around than you think is necessary.

1. Trace or photocopy the paper-piecing pattern. Firmly fold the pattern along *all* of the lines before starting.

2. Follow the number sequence on the pattern when piecing. To begin, place fabric piece #1, wrong side up, on your cutting mat. Pin the paper pattern, drawn side up, to the fabric with piece #1 centered in place underneath. Don't put the pin on the stitchline. Hold the paper up to the light to be sure the fabric covers all of area #1, with generous seam allowances overlapping the lines.

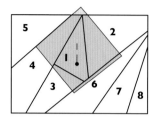

3. Fold the pattern back at the stitching line between the #1 and #2 areas. Trim the fabric to a ¼˝ seam allowance with a ruler and rotary cutter. Unfold the paper pattern.

4. Cut piece #2 large enough to cover the #2 area, with a generous seam allowance. Align the fabric edge of piece #2 with the trimmed seam allowance of fabric piece #1, right sides together, and pin.

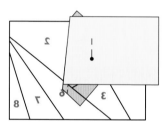

5. Turn the paper over so that you can see the stitch line between areas #1 and #2, and stitch on this line. Start ¼˝ before the start of the line and end ¼˝ beyond the end of it.

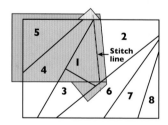

6. Open piece #2 and press.

7. Repeat Steps 3–6 for each piece, working in numerical order.

8. Remove the paper. Press, but do not trim.

appliqué

I fuse or glue a design, then machine appliqué for the postcards. I use appliqué or zigzag stitch on the edge of some design elements, while other elements are free-motion stitched to add depth and definition. The free-motion embroidery done on the leaves and branch of *Juicy!* (see Appliqué on page 35) add definition.

embroidery

As with almost any technique, there is more than one way to present an embroidered design on a fabric postcard. *April Showers Bring May Flowers* (see Embroidery on page 40) includes a small built-in design from an embroidery machine, while *Flowers Brighten the Bluest Day* (see Variations on page 42) features hand embroidery. Don't forget about the possibility of using a scrap of vintage work you've been caring for, like I did on *Gramma Would Be Proud* (see Introduction: Art in the Mail on page 3) and *Grandmother's Roses* (see Photo Printing on page 28). Although technically Broderie Perse, there is embroidery on both flowers.

Angelina

If you haven't met this exciting fiber yet, let me introduce you. Angelina fibers are made of a co-polyester and acrylic core with a co-polyester outer layer. Fibers are about 4 inches long and have a velvet-soft hand. They are available in a rainbow of colors that are fusible at low temperatures and add an iridescent sparkle to everything they touch. They also come in a few metallic colors, which are not fusible but can be mixed sparingly with fusible fibers for extra punch (see Sources on page 47).

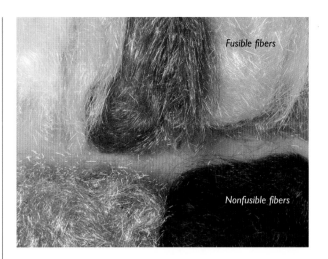

Fusible fibers

Nonfusible fibers

Once fused (complete instructions follow), Angelina sheets can be layered, stitched on, cut into shapes for use in fiber arts, or even painted. In short, they can be treated like a piece of fabric. Have You Met Angelina? (see pages 43–46) will get you started. After you have confidence with fusing the fibers, you'll be prepared to sandwich embellishments (see *Counterpoint* under Variations on page 46); fuse using a rubber stamp or wooden block (see *Heart in Hand* under Variations on page 46); and fuse, cut, and fuse again to create a unique sheet of fabric (see *Angelina in a Maze* under Variations on page 46). For more detailed instructions on these techniques and even more possibilities, see Suggested Reading on page 47.

Fusing Angelina

1. Set the iron for silk, or medium heat.

2. Place a Teflon sheet or parchment paper on the ironing board. Sprinkle Angelina fibers to cover the area size desired.

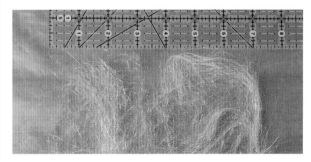

Sprinkle Angelina fibers to cover area size desired.

3. Fold the Teflon sheet to completely cover fibers.

4. Apply iron to top of Teflon sheet, moving over entire area of fibers, for 1–2 seconds. *Caution: If the fibers are fused at too high a temperature or for too long, they will completely lose their sparkle and become a flat color.*

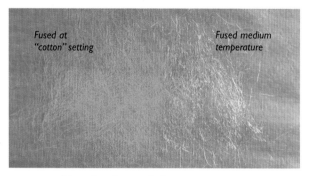

Fused at "cotton" setting

Fused medium temperature

Fibers fused at too high a temperature or for too long will lose their sparkle.

5. Let fibers cool completely before peeling off the Teflon sheet.

fun!

There is no "right" amount of Angelina fibers to use for fusing. The amount used will depend on the effect you want to achieve. Swirl a small amount of fibers, taking care to have overlaps between fibers, for a delicate look, or pile the fibers thickly for dense coverage.

Delicate swirls

Dense coverage

Note: Dense coverage may require that you fuse both sides of the Angelina to ensure complete fusing.

easy!

Use a rag to gather Angelina fragments from your work surface onto one half of the Teflon sheet. Cover fibers with the other half of the Teflon sheet and fuse. Use this small sheet of fibers as inspiration for your next postcard.

assembling the postcard

When you have completed the project instructions, refer to this section to assemble the postcard. Refer to The Filling (see pages 6–7) for more details on the individual fillings discussed here.

Steps for assembling the postcard are determined by whether you handwrite or print your message and address. Use fabric that will coordinate with the design side of the postcard and will provide a high contrast between the fabric color and the writing or printing.

Assembling the Postcard when Handwriting the Message and Address

The assembly is very easy when you are handwriting the back. In a nutshell, you will fuse the 3 layers together, trim to size, and write your message! Here are the detailed directions:

1. If you use fast2fuse for the filling, follow the manufacturer's instructions to fuse the wrong side of the address-side fabric to the fast2fuse. If you use another filling, follow the manufacturer's instructions to fuse paper-backed fusible web to the wrong side of the address-side fabric, and then fuse to the filling.

2. Following the manufacturer's instructions from Step 1, fuse the design side of the postcard to the opposite side of the filling. Don't forget to protect delicate fabrics or embellishments with a Teflon sheet or pressing cloth.

3. Use the viewfinder to determine the design area of the postcard. Mark the 4″ × 6″ area with a marker of your choice. Remember, your binding will cover ¼″ around the entire outside of the design. Make sure critical design elements are not within ¼″ of the edge.

4. Trim on the marked lines.

5. Use a permanent-ink pen to write the message and address.

Yellow fabric allows high contrast for handwritten address and message. Sharon's choice of stamp fits with the modern design of *Time Travel* (see Variations on page 27).

Printing the Message and Address

Refer to Printing on Fabric (see page 29) for complete instructions. Here are a few examples of effective ways to use your printer for the address side of the postcard.

Printed address and message allow space for additional art and signature. Margarete Steinhauer's stamp fits the design of *Ode to a Jeweled Jelly* (see Variations on page 39).

Address and message are printed on white fabric, fused to address-side fabric, and stitched. The stamp becomes part of the design of *Primavera* (see Variations on page 39).

Pieced scraps function as address-side fabric, and printing on white fabric creates high contrast for readability. Ellen used the same stitching for both sides of *Labels* (see Variations on page 34).

Assembling the Postcard with Printed Message and Address

So you don't inadvertently trim off your printed words, you need to trim the front and back of the postcard separately, following these directions:

1. Use the viewfinder to select the design area of the postcard. Mark the 4″ × 6″ area with a marker of your choice. Remember, your binding will cover ¼″ around the outside of the design. Make sure critical design elements are not within ¼″ of the edge.

Select and mark design area, allowing ¼″ around the outside for binding.

2. If you use fast2fuse for the filling, follow the manufacturer's instructions to fuse the design-side fabric to the fast2fuse. If you use another filling, follow the manufacturer's instructions to fuse paper-backed fusible web to the wrong side of the design-side fabric, and then fuse to the filling.

Don't forget to protect delicate fabrics or embellishments with a Teflon sheet or pressing cloth.

3. Trim on the marked lines.

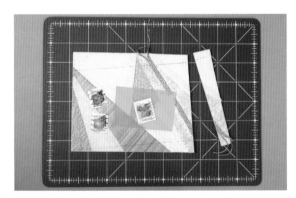

Trim.

4. Trim the printed address side to 4″ × 6″.

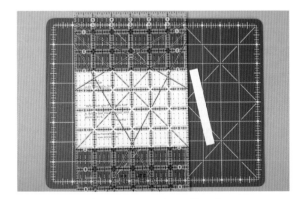

Trim address side to 4″ × 6″.

5. Remove the paper backing and fuse to the other side of the filling.

getting on the edge

The three methods used to finish the edges of the project postcards are satin stitch, stitch-and-fuse binding, and mock-miter binding. A satin-stitch edge can look every bit as crisp as a fabric binding (see *Let the Stitches Speak* on page 23 and *No Envelope* under Collage on page 30). Stitch-and-fuse binding is a faster alternative to traditional mock-miter binding. I like the tailored look it achieves in less time (see *Sun Spots* under Have You Met Angelina? on page 43 and *Grandmother's Roses* under Photo Printing on page 28). Some designs seem to demand the extra effort of mock-miter binding. I used this style for *April Showers Bring May Flowers* (see Embroidery on page 40) and *Juicy!* (see Appliqué on page 35).

Of course, there are many more ways to finish an edge.

A. *Time Travel* (page 27) is bound with fabric strips fused to the front of the card and then pulled over the edge and fused to the address side. The uneven framing that this technique produces is perfect for the style of the postcard.

B. *Ode to a Jeweled Jelly* (page 39) is bound with a traditional quilt binding, minus the miter corners.

C. *Montmartre Doorway* (page 30) wraps the "frame" on the front of the postcard to the address side.

D. *Flowers Brighten the Bluest Day* (page 42) has a satin-stitch edge with yarn straight stitched on top of it.

E. *Angelina in a Maze* (page 46) adds another design feature by satin stitching rickrack on the edge.

F. *Lake Superior, Marquette, Michigan* (page 30) has a decorative ladder stitch for its binding.

A. Uneven fused fabric binding

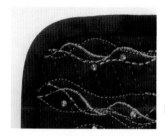

B. Traditional binding, rounded corners

C. Fabric frame wraps to address side and is fused in place.

D. Yarn stitched on top of satin-stitch edge

E. Rickrack edge

F. Decorative-stitch edge

These are just a few of the possibilities! You'll think of many more as you begin making the postcards. Below are the three methods used for the projects.

Satin Stitch

Stitching around the card twice is the key to a secure satin-stitch edge. Use a normal length and a narrow-width zigzag stitch the first time around the postcard. This captures the edge and any details that need to be secured. Use a short length and a wider-width satin stitch the second time around to complete a smooth edge.

1. Select a 30- or 40-weight thread to coordinate with your design and the same weight thread to coordinate with your address side. If you are using a metallic thread for one side, consider a cotton thread of the same weight for the other side. Attach the appliqué foot. (If you don't have an appliqué foot, use a foot you're comfortable with, such as an open-toe appliqué foot or an even-feed foot.)

2. Select the zigzag stitch on the sewing machine. Determine the width to be used for the second stitching (final edge), and set your stitch width narrower than that. Use the default or normal stitch length.

3. Begin at any corner, and stitch so that when the needle swings to the right it falls just off the edge of the postcard. This will "capture" the edge of the postcard, encasing any loose fabric, thread, or embellishment. Stitch all four sides in this manner.

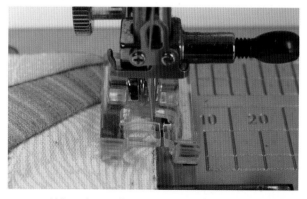

When the needle swings to the right, it should fall just off the edge of the postcard.

4. Reset the stitch width to allow complete coverage of the first zigzag stitching. Reset the stitch length to be short enough to completely cover the fabric with thread as you stitch. Test the stitch length and machine tension on the test scrap (see Fun! on page 10) you have handy.

5. Begin stitching at any corner, and be sure the needle falls just off the edge of the postcard when it swings to the right.

Final stitch width is wider than first stitching and covers fabric completely. Needle falls just off the right edge.

6. Use a locking stitch or back tack on the left swing of the needle to secure the binding.

Stitch-and-Fuse Binding

This binding looks every bit as neat and tailored as the mock-miter binding but is much quicker. You will be sewing the binding to the design side of the postcard and then fusing the binding to the back.

1. From the binding fabric, cut 2 strips 1″ × 6½″ and 2 strips 1″ × 5″.

2. From the paper-backed fusible web, cut 2 strips ½″ × 6½″ and 2 strips ½″ × 5″.

3. Following the manufacturer's instructions, fuse the paper-backed fusible web to one edge on the wrong side of the same-size fabric strips.

4. On the design side of the postcard, center 1 long binding strip on one long side of the postcard, with right sides together and the edge without the fusible aligned with the postcard edge. Stitch using a ¼″ seam allowance. Repeat for the opposite side of the postcard.

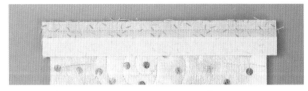

Center 6½″ binding strip and stitch using ¼″ seam allowance.

5. Remove the paper backing on the fusible web. Wrap the binding strip over the edge of the postcard, pulling it snug, and hold firmly as you fuse the binding in place on the address side. The binding will cover the stitching. Repeat for the other side.

Wrap binding to the address side, holding firmly as you fuse.

6. Trim excess binding fabric even with the postcard.

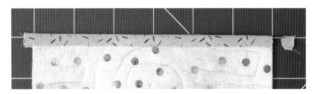

Trim binding even with postcard.

7. Center 1 short binding strip on one short end of the postcard, with right sides together and the edge without the fusible aligned with the postcard edge. Stitch using a ¼″ seam allowance. Repeat for the other short side of the postcard.

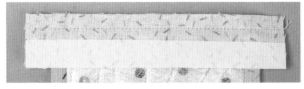

Center 5″ binding strips on short ends of postcard and stitch using ¼″ seam allowance.

8. Place the postcard with the address side up. Use sharp-pointed scissors to trim a part of a corner of the binding away. Begin on the unstitched side of the binding, and cut even with the long postcard side, stopping at the edge of the postcard. Turn scissors parallel to the short edge of the postcard, and trim away the fabric. This will leave a small tab of fabric on the edge of the postcard. Repeat for the opposite end of the binding.

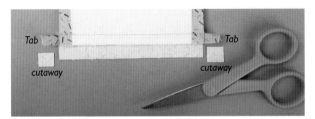

Cut even with the long side, stopping at edge of postcard. Turn scissors parallel to short edge, and trim away the fabric.

9. Repeat Step 8 for the other short side.

10. Remove the paper backing. Pull the fabric tab firmly over the edge of the postcard and pin it in place. Repeat for second tab.

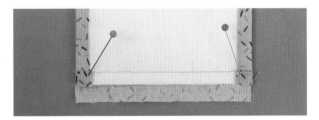

Pull tabs firmly over edge and pin.

11. Pull the binding over the edge of the postcard and hold it firmly in place as you fuse the binding edge in place. The binding will cover the fabric tab and the stitching.

Pull binding over edge; hold firmly as you fuse.

12. Remove the pins.

13. Repeat Steps 10–12 for the other short side.

Mock-Miter Binding

Continuous bias binding is easier to apply to the rigid postcard than binding strips cut on the straight of grain.

1. Cut a 7″ × 7″ square of binding fabric on a 45° angle into 1¼″-wide strips.

2. Stitch the strips together at right angles; trim excess fabric, leaving a ¼″ seam allowance; and press the seams open.

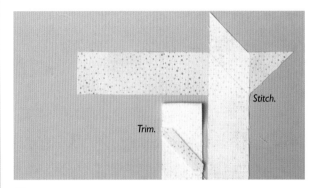

3. With the raw edges even and the right sides of fabric together, lay the binding along the entire edge of one long edge of the postcard's design side. Using a ¼″ seam allowance, begin stitching about 2″ from the bottom corner of the postcard, and stop stitching ¼″ from the corner. Backstitch.

Stop ¼″ from corner, backstitch.

4. Remove the postcard from the machine, trim the threads, and rotate one-quarter turn. Fold the binding at a right angle so it extends straight above the postcard.

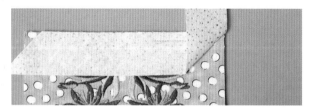

Fold binding up.

5. Fold the binding strip down, even with the edge of the postcard. This creates the corner miter. Resume stitching, mitering each corner as you come to it.

Fold binding down and resume stitching at edge.

6. Stop stitching about 2″ after you turn the last corner. Backstitch. Remove postcard and cut threads. Measure a 1¼″ overlap and trim the excess binding.

7. Lay the postcard design side up. Place the unstitched tails of binding at right angles and pin. Draw a line from the upper right corner to the lower left corner of the binding as shown. Hand stitch the final seam.

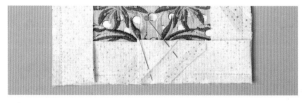

Place tails at right angles and pin. Draw a line and handstitch.

8. Trim the diagonal seam allowance to ¼″ and finger-press the seam open. Finish machine stitching the binding to the postcard.

9. Turn the binding to the address side of the postcard. Turn under ¼″ of binding and hand stitch the binding, mitering each corner as you come to it. The binding should cover the stitching line.

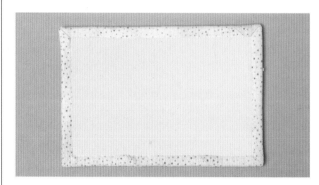

Turn under binding and hand stitch.

let the stitches
speak

This fun project will have you playing with utility and decorative stitches in new ways.

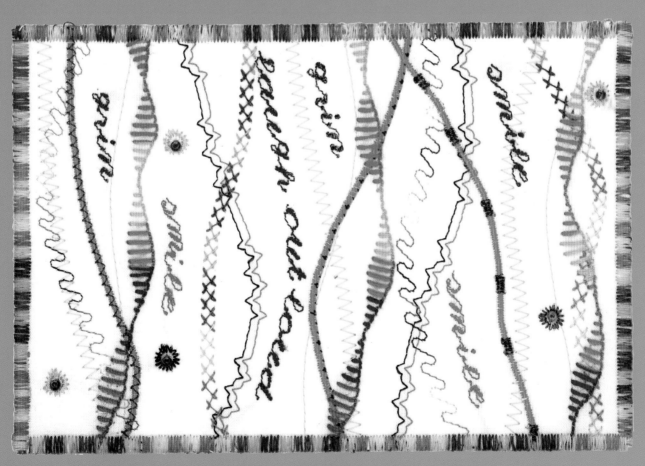

Let the Stitches Speak

You will need a sewing machine with decorative stitches to make this project. The machine does not have to stitch the words. I like to do my stitching on a fat quarter and cut it up before I add the words. Each card is unique but related.

What You'll Need

- ☐ 1 rectangle 5″ × 7″ of white fabric for design
- ☐ 1 rectangle 5″ × 7″ of coordinating fabric for address side*
- ☐ 40-wt. decorative thread in yellow, golden yellow, orange, blue, purple, dark green, and variegated green
- ☐ 40-wt. cotton thread, variegated green
- ☐ metallic thread, green
- ☐ jean stitch cotton thread, variegated with 3 or 4 colors
- ☐ bobbin thread for decorative stitching
- ☐ 40-wt. decorative thread for satin-stitch binding (Use the same thread in the bobbin or a thread to coordinate with the address-side fabric.)

- ☐ Nymo beading thread in a color to match the beads or a neutral (see page 8)
- ☐ 1 rectangle 5″ × 7″ of Pellon Shirtailor fusible nonwoven interfacing for stabilizer (see Stabilizer on page 6)
- ☐ 1 rectangle 5″ × 7″ of fast2fuse (see page 6 for substitute)
- ☐ topstitch 80/12 or Microtex sharp needle
- ☐ topstitch 90/14 or Jeans needle
- ☐ metallica needle
- ☐ 2.0 twin needle
- ☐ 5 beads

*If you use your computer to print a message and/or address, you will also need:

- ☐ 1 rectangle 5″ × 7″ of paper-backed fusible web for address-side fabric

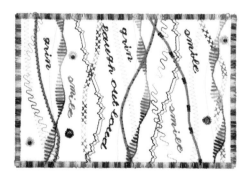

How-Tos

Gently curving lines are more interesting than straight lines. Slowly move the fabric to the right and back to the left while stitching.

1. Press the 5″ × 7″ white fabric for the design side.

2. Following the manufacturer's instructions, fuse the Shirtailor to the wrong side of the fabric.

3. Insert the topstitch 80/12 or Microtex sharp needle and thread the machine with yellow decorative thread.

4. Visually divide the width of the fabric into 3 areas. This does not have to be exact, so don't bother drawing lines. Use a straight stitch and a slow, steady speed to sew a curving line in the first third of the fabric. Repeat in the remaining 2 areas of the fabric.

5. Set the machine for a moderately wide zigzag (I set 4.0) and the default stitch length. Stitch 3 curving lines on the fabric, letting one or more of the zigzag lines cross over the straight-stitch line.

6. Replace the topstitch needle with the 2.0 twin needle, and thread the machine with 40-wt. decorative threads in dark green and orange. Choose a decorative stitch. Program the machine to stitch it 3 times followed by a straight stitch 3 times.

easy!

If your machine will not allow multiple-stitch programming, either stop after each stitch has been sewn 3 times and reset the type of stitch OR stitch with a decorative stitch only.

7. Visually divide the fabric into 2 areas. Stitch 2 curved lines of twin needle decorative stitches.

8. Replace the 2.0 twin needle with the topstitch needle from Step 3, and thread the machine with the orange decorative thread. Set the machine for a narrow zigzag and a short length. I set my machine for 2.0/.35. Stitch 3 curved lines, allowing 2 of the lines to overlap each other and/or other stitches.

9. Replace the topstitch needle with a metallica needle, and thread the machine with green metallic thread. Set the machine for a slightly wider zigzag (I set my machine for 2.5 width) and the default stitch length. Overstitch 1 of the lines of orange zigzag stitching (left in the photo). Be sure to stitch slowly and steadily so that you remain exactly over the orange line.

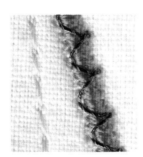

Maintain a slow, steady speed to remain exactly over the orange line as you overstitch.

10. Maintain the stitch width from Step 9, and adjust the stitch length to a shorter length (I set my length for .35). Overstitch another line of orange with random intervals of satin stitch (right in the photo).

11. Create dots with this overstitch technique.

The tightened top tension, coupled with the loosened tension of the bobbin case, will pull the bobbin thread to the top of the fabric, creating tiny dots. A high contrast in thread colors is important.

Select blanket stitch. Adjust width to a very narrow setting, and lengthen the stitch a moderate length. (I set my machine at 1.0/3.0) Wind a bobbin with the dark green decorative thread, and loosen the tension of your second bobbin case (see Bobbin Case on page 10). (I set my bobbin tension at 11 o'clock. My factory-set bobbin is at 1 o'clock.) Insert the needle from Step 3. Thread the machine with the orange decorative thread, and tighten the upper tension. (I set my machine at 8 to 9; normal tension is 2 to 3.) If you have the needle-down feature on your machine, select it. Experiment with this technique on your test scrap (Fun! page 10) to discover the tension settings you need. Insert your machine needle exactly on the right edge of the last orange line. Stitch slowly and steadily, keeping your stitching line exactly on the right edge of the orange line.

Stitch exactly on the right edge of the orange line.

fun!

Stitch the dots again on your scrap fabric. This time, widen the zigzag stitch of your initial line. Use a heavier-weight thread, say 30-weight cotton or jeans stitch, to create the dots. Remember to use the same weight thread in the bobbin and top, but with high contrast in colors.

12. Replace the loosened bobbin with your factory-set bobbin case. Reset the upper tension to normal for your machine. Select a decorative stitch, and thread the machine with decorative thread in variegated green. I chose an S-curve decorative stitch. Set the machine for a moderately wide stitch and a shorter length (I set my machine at 5.0/2.0). Stitch 2 lines, making sure that each line overlaps 1 or 2 previously stitched lines.

13. Select another decorative stitch, and thread the machine with cotton thread in variegated green. I chose a crosshatch stitch. This is normally a very wide stitch (7.0), so I narrowed it to 4.0 and set a stitch length of 2.0. Stitch 2 lines, making sure that each line overlaps 1 or 2 previously stitched lines.

14. Thread the machine with the variegated jeans stitch thread, and select the blanket stitch. Set the stitch for maximum width and minimum length (I set my machine for 7.0/1.0). While stitching a steady, curving line, reduce the width of the stitch to the lowest setting possible. Immediately begin increasing the width to the maximum setting possible.

Continue stitching and adjusting to complete the line of curvy stitching that looks like a ribbon.

15. Use the viewfinder to select the design area you like (see Basic Tools on page 9). Keep in mind that the next stitching will be the words in this design. Allow room for the words and ¼˝ around the outside of the design area for the binding. Draw the desired 4˝ × 6˝ design area.

16. Program the words *grin, smile,* and *laugh out loud,* and stitch in purple, red, and green decorative threads.

easy!

If your machine doesn't stitch letters, write the words with permanent-ink pens in appropriate colors.

17. Select an eyelet stitch, and stitch in golden yellow and blue decorative threads.

embellish

Attach beads in the center of the eyelet stitches with 2 stitches per bead, using Nymo thread.

assemble the card

Refer to Assembling the Postcard (see page 16) for complete instructions.

finish the edge

Add a satin-stitch binding, following the instructions on page 19.

Variations

A. Use your free-motion embroidery skills with zigzag stitch to create this heart-felt card. Cut a heart from a dark red fabric, draw lines to divide it into four sections, and fuse it to your design fabric. Stitch each section in one direction, then pivot and stitch a second time in the opposite direction to get complete coverage.

B. A bag of "flossing threads" (see easy! and fun! tips on page XX) inspired *Time Travel*, made by Sharon Benton. Black netting was placed on top, and the surface was free-motion stitched moving around the wire.

C. Here's a quick recipe for *Spring Greens*: Sandwich snips of fabric between water-soluble stabilizer (bottom) and tulle (top). Free-motion stitch with a variety of weights and types of thread, using straight and zigzag stitches. Place this on top of the fabric, and stitch a grid to secure. Rinse the stabilizer, leaving some behind to "keep the greens crisp."

D. Zigzag a plaid postcard in no time. Draw lines to stitch on, or use your quilting bar attached to the even-feed foot.

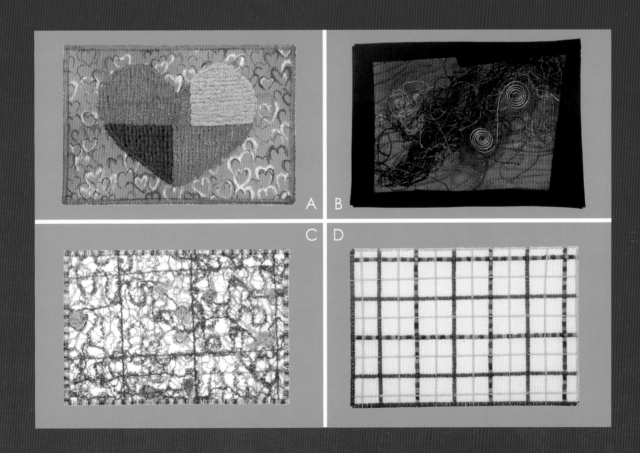

photo printing

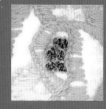

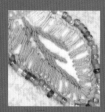

The photograph used for *Grandmother's Roses* was taken on her wedding day and is one of my favorite photographs of her. I have used one of the Broderie Perse roses she stitched on a tablecloth to echo the silk roses on her dress. Other small, sentimental items (such as a portion of a letter or handkerchief) could also be used.

Grandmother's Roses

What You'll Need

- [ ] 1 rectangle 4½″ × 7″ white fabric for printing the photograph
- [ ] 1 rectangle 5″ × 7″ small-scale print for design background
- [ ] 1 rectangle 5″ × 7″ coordinating fabric for the address side*
- [ ] 1 rectangle 6″ × 7″ coordinating fabric for binding
- [ ] 1 rectangle 5″ × 7″ Pellon Shirtailor fusible non woven interfacing for stabilizer (see Stabilizer on page 6)
- [ ] 1 rectangle 7″ × 10″ paper-backed fusible web for photo, sentimental item, and binding
- [ ] assorted seed beads in colors to coordinate with the sentimental item of choice (optional)
- [ ] #5 perle cotton thread in two shades of a color to coordinate with the sentimental item
- [ ] thread to coordinate with the design (I have used black thread to suggest a frame and bring out the black floss used in the center of the rose.)
- [ ] Nymo beading thread in a color to match the beads or in a neutral (see Nymo Beading Thread on page 8)
- [ ] 1 rectangle 5″ × 7″ fast2fuse (see page 6 for substitute)
- [ ] photograph
- [ ] sentimental item
- [ ] Bubble Jet Set (see Fabric Preparation on page 12)

*If you use your computer to print a message and/or address, you will also need:

- [ ] 1 rectangle 5″ × 7″ paper-backed fusible web for address-side fabric

How-Tos

prepare fabric for printing

My DeskJet (HP) printer, as well as the Bubble Jet (Canon), Apple, Epson, and other ink-jet printers, uses a water-soluble ink. This means that the printed image will not be permanent, so if it becomes wet, the ink will run. If thoroughly moistened, the image will disappear. Follow the manufacturer's directions on Bubble Jet Set to prepare your fabric for printing to ensure that the printed image is permanent.

printing the photograph

Refer to Printing on Fabric on page 12 for complete instructions.

Note: White fabric is the best choice for printing a photograph because the fabric will show through any open or white areas of your photograph.

Trim the printed photograph to desired size and shape. My photograph is an oval, 2½″ × 3⅛″.

assembling the design

1. Following the manufacturer's instructions, fuse the Shirtailor to the wrong side of the small-scale print fabric.

2. Following the manufacturer's instructions, fuse paper-backed fusible web to the wrong side of the sentimental item. Trim to size and shape.

3. Remove the paper backing on the printed photograph and the sentimental item.

4. Position the photograph and the sentimental item on the small-scale print fabric. Try a number of orientations and angles. Use the viewfinder (see Basic Tools on page 9) to help establish the best placement. Remove the sentimental item, and fuse the photograph in place.

5. Stitch around the photograph with pearl cotton, using a cording stitch and foot to couch the perle cotton threads. I used a triple cording stitch so the outer stitch, without perle cotton thread, would create the look of an old-fashioned frame.

6. Position the sentimental item again. Use the viewfinder to be sure you are happy with the placement. Fuse in place.

embellish

Attach beads with 2 stitches per bead, using Nymo thread.

assembling the card

Refer to Assembling the Postcard (see page 16) for complete instructions.

finishing the edge

Add a stitch-and-fuse binding, following the instructions on page 20.

Variations

A. Use your city map, or download a map from an Internet source and print. You're sure to get a fast RSVP when you send this invitation out!

B. Photos were printed, cut out, and fused to fabric already covered with Angelina fibers. Bugle beads and variegated thread finish *Suitcase 2/10* made by Jenni Paige.

C. Brick sidewalk and building details are brought out with a black Pigma pen and free-motion quilting. *Montmartre Doorway* was made by Sharon Benton.

D. This photograph is printed on photo paper, trimmed, and stitched to fabric with gold metallic thread. Janice Simpson made *Lake Superior, Marquette, Michigan*.

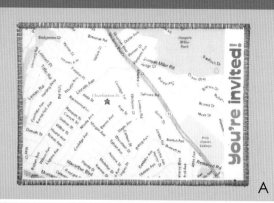

A | B

C | D

collage

One of the official rules of Postmark'd Art and art2mail (the two groups I trade postcards with) is that you cannot use an envelope to mail the postcard. So how about putting one on the postcard as part of a collage? I call it *No Envelope*. What collage themes appeal to you?

No Envelope

What You'll Need

- ☐ 8 scraps of neutral fabric for paper-pieced back ground
- ☐ 1 rectangle 5″ × 7″ coordinating fabric for address side*
- ☐ 1 rectangle 5″ × 7″ Pellon Shirtailor fusible non woven interfacing for stabilizer (see Stabilizer on page 6)
- ☐ 1 envelope, paper or vellum, smaller than the postcard (see Sources on page 47)
- ☐ 4 cancelled stamps
- ☐ 18″ of 1/16″ ribbon (I used rayon ribbon for hand embroidery from Oliver Twists, color No. 002)

- ☐ thread to match the ribbon for couching (I used thread from the Oliver Twists collection above) and for binding
- ☐ 1 scrap paper-backed fusible web for the envelope and stamps
- ☐ 1 rectangle 5″ × 7″ fast2fuse (see page 6 for substitute)

*If you use your computer to print a message and/or address, you will also need:

- ☐ 1 rectangle 5″ × 7″ paper-backed fusible web for address-side fabric

How-Tos

paper piecing

I like the added dimension that the paper-pieced background gives to this postcard; however, you could also use a single piece of fabric. Refer to page 14 for complete instructions on paper piecing. Use the paper-piecing pattern on page 33.

fast!

Add items to the collage by using a fabric with pencils and/or pens printed on it as part of the background.

assembling the collage

1. Use the photograph as a guide to couch the ribbon with a zigzag stitch to the lower left corner of the post-card. Check stitch width on a piece of scrap fabric first. The needle should fall exactly on the outside edges of the rib-bon.

Needle should fall exactly on outside edges of ribbon.

fun!

Use cording, rickrack, yarn, or decorative stitches in place of the ribbon to personalize your postcard.

2. Following the manufacturer's instructions, fuse paper-backed fusible web to the envelope front and the wrong side of each cancelled stamp.

3. Position the envelope and 3 stamps on the post-card.

4. Use the viewfinder to select the design area you like. Allow room for the 1/4″ binding. Draw the desired 4″ × 6″ design area. Fuse the envelope and stamps into place.

5. Lift the envelope flap back, and stitch a straight line just below the fold of the flap. Reduce your stitch length if necessary.

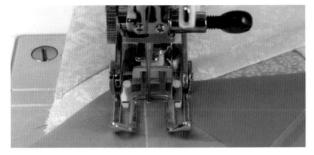

Stitch just below fold line.

6. Replace the envelope flap. Seal the envelope by fusing the final stamp on the back.

assembling the card

Refer to Assembling the Postcard (see page 16) for complete instructions.

finishing the edge

Refer to Satin Stitch (see page 19) for complete instructions.

easy!

Use an envelope you can see through. Tuck a message inside and seal the envelope with a sticker!

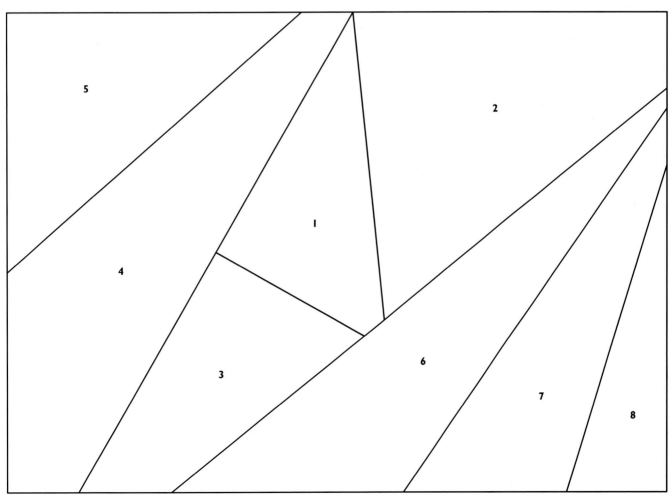

Paper-piecing pattern

Variations

A. Kathie Briggs captured handmade and Japanese papers under tulle to create *Kimono Ladies and Fans*. Straight and decorative stitches secure the layers.

B. Recycle clothing labels. The company names and colors of the labels can help determine the recipient of the postcard. *Labels* was created by Ellen Slattery.

C. *Care Instructions* recycles those small labels found inside your garments that tell you how to care for the garment once you get it home.

D. Capture watch findings (see Sources on page 47) under tulle and send *Time in a Bottle* to someone who needs more time in their day! A narrow strip of cheesecloth creates the light source on the bottle.

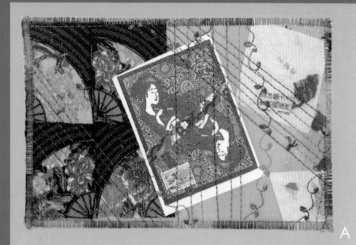

A B

C D

appliqué

Add some texture to a simple appliqué design with a scrap of batting and some stitching. These backyard beauties really do look *Juicy*! No need to fret if the oranges aren't all shaped exactly alike—I don't think nature worries about such uniformity.

Juicy

What You'll Need

- [ ] 1 scrap 3″ × 6″ solid orange fabric for oranges
- [ ] 1 scrap 2″ × 4″ light green fabric for leaves
- [ ] 1 square 5″ × 5″ medium green fabric for branch and leaves
- [ ] 1 rectangle 5″ × 7″ purple-dotted fabric for design background AND
- [ ] 1 square 7″ × 7″ purple-dotted fabric for binding
- [ ] 1 rectangle 5″ × 7″ coordinating fabric for address side (you could use the solid orange fabric)*
- [ ] Thread to blend with fabrics: 1 orange, 1 light green, 1 medium green
- [ ] 1 rectangle 5″ × 7″ Pellon Shirtailor fusible non woven interfacing for stabilizer (see Stabilizer on page 6)
- [ ] 1 rectangle fast2fuse; 5″ × 7″ (see page 6 for substitute)
- [ ] 1 scrap 3″ × 6″ thin cotton batting
- [ ] 2 pieces 2″ × 4″, 5″ × 5″ paper-backed fusible web
- [ ] blue water-soluble marking pen
- [ ] fabric glue
- [ ] mini pressing iron (optional)
- [ ] stiletto or seam ripper

*If you use your computer to print a message and/or address, you will also need:

- [ ] 1 rectangle 5″ × 7″ paper-backed fusible web for address-side fabric

How-Tos

1. Trace branch pattern and 4 leaf patterns onto 1 piece of paper-backed fusible web. Trace 4 more leaves onto another piece of the paper-backed fusible web. Leave about ¼″ space around all pattern pieces.

2. Following the manufacturers' instructions, fuse the branch and 4 leaves to the wrong side of the medium green fabric. Fuse the remaining 4 leaves to the wrong side of the light green fabric.

3. Cut out patterns on the lines and set aside.

4. Following the manufacturer's instructions, fuse Pellon Shirtailor to the wrong side of the purple-dotted fabric. Set aside.

making the oranges

1. Use a pencil to trace 3 orange patterns (patterns on page 38) directly onto the orange fabric. If needed, use a lightbox, or copy and tape the pattern to a window for tracing.

2. Use a blue water-soluble marking pen to trace the stitching lines on each orange.

Trace orange pattern with a pencil and stitching lines with a blue water-soluble marking pen.

3. Place the orange fabric on top of the batting.

4. Reduce the stitch length to 18–20 stitches per inch. Thread the machine with orange thread.

5. Stitch the 2 circles at the top of the orange.

6. Stitch the remaining horizontal lines, beginning and ending stitches outside the pattern lines.

7. Stitch vertical lines in the same manner, beginning and ending stitches outside the pattern lines where possible.

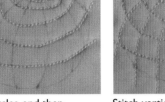

Stitch circles, and then horizontal lines

Stitch vertical lines.

8. Divide vertical lines in half and stitch again. Continue dividing and stitching until stitch lines are about ⅛˝ apart.

9. Repeat Step 8 for the horizontal lines.

Orange completely stitched

10. Repeat Steps 5–9 for the remaining 2 oranges.

11. Place the stitched oranges in hot water for about 10 minutes. Let dry flat. This will produce a slightly puckered texture, and it will wash out the blue ink.

12. Cut out the oranges on the perimeter pencil pattern lines.

assembling the design

1. Remove the paper backing on the branch and leaf patterns.

2. Using the photo as a guide, place the pattern pieces on the purple-dotted background fabric. Use the viewfinder to help determine the best placement and to ensure that you have left ¼˝ around the entire design for binding.

3. When you are satisfied with the design placement, remove the 3 oranges and the light leaf on top of the 2 oranges.

Remove the oranges and one leaf; check ¼˝ allowance.

4. Fuse the remaining pattern pieces in place, taking care not to fuse the branch node on the underside of the branch (you will tuck an orange under the node later). Use a seam ripper or stiletto to raise the node off the fabric as you press the branch.

Use a seam ripper or stiletto to lift node as you press.

5. Dot the edges of the wrong side of one orange with fabric glue. Lift the branch node and tuck the orange under the node.

6. Dot the wrong side of the remaining 2 oranges with fabric glue and place them on the design. Allow the glue to dry.

7. Replace the last leaf on the design. Fuse the node of the branch and the leaf into place.

easy!

This mini iron makes pressing and fusing very small areas a breeze. If you don't have one, use the tip of your iron.

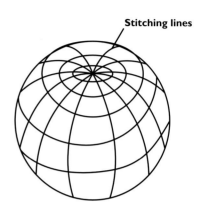

8. Use the medium green thread to free-motion stitch the very edge of the branch OR appliqué the edges with a narrow zigzag stitch.

9. Use medium green thread to free-motion embroider the 4 medium green leaves OR appliqué the edges with a narrow zigzag stitch.

10. Repeat Step 9 for the light green leaves, using light green thread.

11. Use the orange thread to appliqué the 3 oranges with a narrow zigzag stitch.

assembling the card

Refer to Assembling the Postcard (see page 16) for complete instructions.

finishing the edge

Add mock-miter binding, following the instructions on page 21.

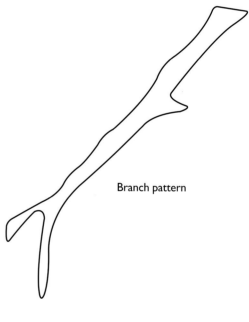

Stitching lines

Orange pattern

Branch pattern

Leaf pattern

Variations

A. Fuse the background to the filling and use a decorative stitch to secure. Fuse and stitch the bowl. Layer ¼″ strips of sheer fabric, and free-motion stitch swirls to hold in place. Add beads for "spice." *Salad for Franki* made by Darma Redwine.

B. Fuse the background to the filling and then fuse the cotton voile jellyfish shape on top. Echo stitching through all layers creates texture and a sense of the water; wavy tentacles (elongated decorative stitches) let you know it's on the move. *Ode to a Jeweled Jelly* made by Margarete Steinhauer.

C. Fuse the background fabric to the filling and free-motion quilt. Cut flower and leaf shapes from Kaffee Fasset fabric, fuse in place, and appliqué (narrow blind stitch gives a thorny appearance). Beads accent each flower. *Primavera* made by Margarete Steinhauer.

D. Stagger ³⁄₈″ strips of orange fabric and fuse to a feather-print fabric to create a fireplace. Couch yarn to put the finishing touch on Santa's hat on *Santa Baby, Hurry Down the Chimney Tonight!* made by Debra Svedberg.

 A

 B

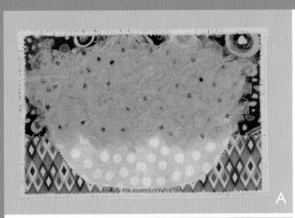 C

 D

embroidery

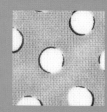

I love embroidery! Today's fabulous embroidery machines make it possible to stitch thousands of designs. *April Showers Bring May Flowers* was made using design #34—one of 47 built-in designs on my Janome 10001. Choose a small design on your machine, find your instruction manual, and start stitching.

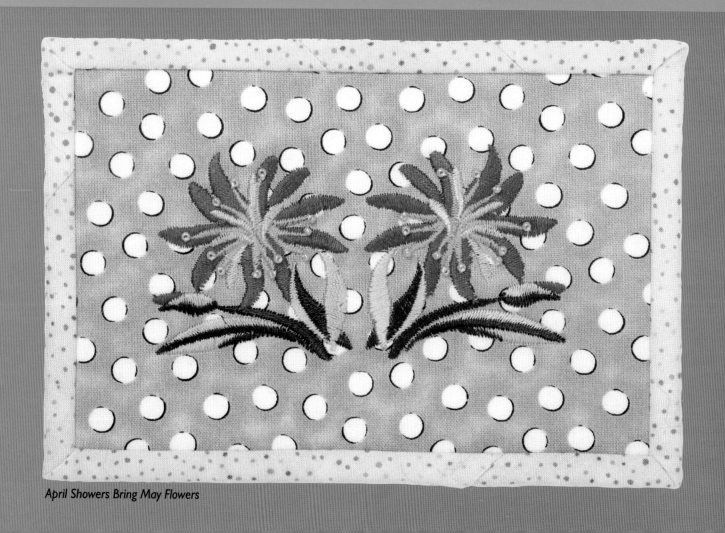

April Showers Bring May Flowers

What You'll Need

- ☐ 1 rectangle fabric for design side (9˝ × 8˝ fits in my hoop; check your hoop size first to determine the size fabric you need)

- ☐ 1 rectangle 5˝ × 7˝ coordinating fabric for address side*

- ☐ 1 square 7˝ × 7˝ complementary fabric for binding

- ☐ Thread colors specified by the embroidery design program

- ☐ Bobbin thread

- ☐ Nymo beading thread in a color to match the beads, or a neutral (see page 8)

- ☐ 1 rectangle Pellon Shirtailor fusible nonwoven interfacing for stabilizer same size as design fabric (see Stabilizer on page 6)

- ☐ 1 rectangle 5˝ × 7˝ fast2fuse (see page 6 for a substitute)

- ☐ embroidery needle

- ☐ beads or other small embellishments (optional)

- ☐ 1 rectangle Sulky Sticky large enough to fit in embroidery hoop (optional)

*If you use your computer to print a message and/or address, you will also need:

- ☐ 1 rectangle 5˝ × 7˝ paper-backed fusible web for address-side fabric

How-Tos

embroider

The flower design of my postcard is 2˝ × 2˝. I duplicated and flipped it, snugging the mirror image alongside the first flower. The resulting 4˝ × 2˝ design fits nicely on the postcard.

1. Press the fabric for the design side.

2. Following the manufacturer's instructions, fuse Shirtailor nonwoven interfacing to the wrong side of the fabric.

3. Secure the stabilized fabric in the embroidery hoop for your machine. The fabric should be taut but not pulled so tightly that it distorts.

4. Stitch the design.

5. Remove the stitched design from the hoop and trim threads.

6. Press with steam to relax the fibers.

If you are experiencing puckering due to stretchy fabric or an intricate design or both, try these tips:

Secure Sulky Sticky (see Sources on page 47) in your embroidery hoop, sticky side up. Place the fabric with the Shirtailor already fused to the wrong side on top of the Sticky. Smooth the fabric. If your embroidery machine has a hoop basting option, use it. If not, sew a line of basting stitching just outside the design stitching area. This does not need to be an exact shape; it just needs to be outside the design stitch area. Stitch the design and remove the basting stitch. Remove the Sticky but leave the Shirtailor in place.

Note: When using Sticky the fabric doesn't need to be hooped, so you can use a 5˝ × 7˝ rectangle of fabric.

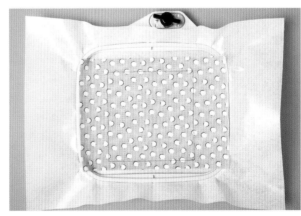

Secure Sticky in the hoop. Place stabilized fabric on top, smoothing wrinkles out, and sew a basting stitch outside design stitching area.

easy!

Stitch your favorite design with a twin needle. The leaf on the left is stitched with a single embroidery needle. The leaf on the right is stitched with a Janome shadow work twin embroidery needle. Check with your dealer about the type of needle you should use.

single needle

twin needle

2.0 shadow-work twin embroidery needle

embellish

Stitch each bead or other small embellishment using Nymo beading thread and 2 stitches.

assembling the card

Refer to Assembling the Postcard (see page 16) for complete instructions.

finishing the edge

Add mock-miter binding, following the instructions on page 21.

Variations

A. Some online embroidery companies sell designs in many formats that will work on your embroidery machine. Many sell individual designs (see Sources on page 47). *We've Moo-ved* is an example.

B. Have your design or a photograph digitized so you can stitch it like in *I Brake for Bichons*. (see Sources on page 47).

C. This postcard combines two individual designs. One daffodil was used 3 times, then the hummingbird was added. Zigzag stitching completes the stems.

D. Free-motion stitching captures yarn between cotton fabric and netting to create the background. Laurie Walton then hand embroidered and beaded *Flowers Brighten the Bluest Day*.

A

B

C

D

have you met Angelina?

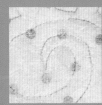

Sun Spots will have you fusing Angelina fibers like an expert in no time. And with the fast and easy stitch-and-fuse binding, you'll want to make several of these at once.

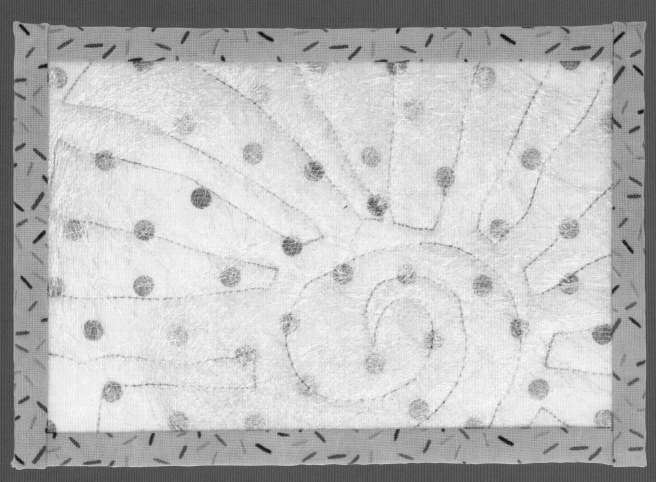

Sun Spots

What You'll Need

- ☐ 1 rectangle 5″ × 7″ white fabric for design

- ☐ 1 rectangle 5″ × 7″ dotted organza for design (a dotted fabric with white background could substitute for the white fabric and dotted organza)

- ☐ 1 rectangle 5″ × 7″ white tulle for design

- ☐ 1 rectangle 5″ × 7″ coordinating fabric for address side*

- ☐ 1 rectangle 5″ × 7″ coordinating fabric for binding

- ☐ Variegated metallic thread, colors to coordinate with dots of organza

- ☐ Angelina fusible fibers, lemon sparkle (see Sources on page 47

- ☐ 1 rectangle 5″ × 7″ fast2fuse (see page 6 for substitute)

- ☐ 1 rectangle 2″ × 7″ paper-backed fusible web for binding

- ☐ 1 rectangle 5″ × 7″ tissue paper (optional)

- ☐ metallica needle

*If you use your computer to print a message and/or address, you will also need:

- ☐ 1 rectangle 5″ × 7″ paper-backed fusible web for address-side fabric

How-Tos

fusing Angelina fibers

Refer to Fusing Angelina (see page 15) for complete instructions. Fuse a thin layer of fibers to cover a 5″ × 7″ area. When fused, the fibers should not form a solid rectangle, but should be placed so that there will be empty space here and there.

> Practice your fusing techniques by creating several "sheets" of the lemon sparkle Angelina or sheets of several different colors. See Variations on page 46 for more possibilities.

assembling the design

1. Following the manufacturer's directions, fuse the white fabric to the fast2fuse.

2. Place the organza, fused Angelina fibers, and white tulle on top of the white fabric, in that order.

3. Pin each corner to secure the layers. The pin does not need to go all the way through the fast2fuse; it just needs to catch the surface to hold all the layers in place.

Pin through all the fabric layers and surface of fast2fuse to secure.

4. Attach the darning foot, insert a metallica needle, and thread the machine with the metallic thread. Free-motion quilt the Sun Quilting Pattern on page 45. When you have a portion of the pattern quilted, you may find it easier to remove the pins and then complete the quilting. OR

Trace the sun pattern onto tissue paper. Place it on top of the white tulle. Pin as described in Step 3, and quilt. Remove tissue paper.

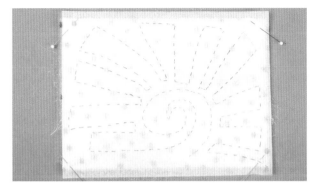

Trace Sun Quilting Pattern on tissue paper. Pin.

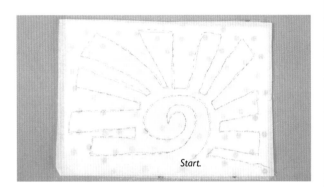

Start.

Quilt.

assembling the postcard

Refer to Assembling the Postcard (see page 16) for complete instructions.

fast!

Instead of fabric, couch a glitzy thread with Mono-Poly or clear nylon thread to finish the edge.

finishing the edge

Add a stitch-and-fuse binding, following the instructions on page 20.

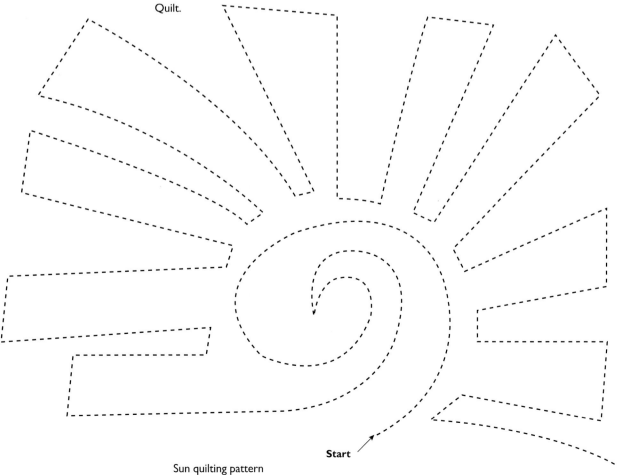

Start

Sun quilting pattern

Variations

A. Use a combination of stitches to create a simple grid that secures the Angelina. Beads are always an option—especially on a *Cloudy Day!*

B. Sandwich embellishments between thin layers of Angelina. Trim to the desired shape. Curved stitching made with twin needles on the background creates a nice *Counterpoint* to the new angular shape of the fused fibers.

C. Use a stamp or wood block, or make your own shapes on which to fuse Angelina. These simple shapes are cut from a sheet of cork for *Heart in Hand*.

D. Use three colors of Angelina to create a fabric sheet. Crosscut the fused sheet of fibers and rearrange the strips. Fuse again to create a single sheet. Finish the edge by satin stitching rickrack in place, and you have *Angelina in a Maze*.

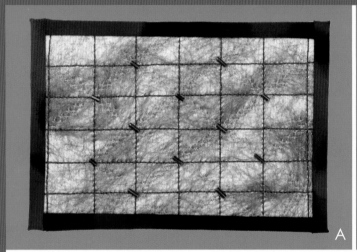
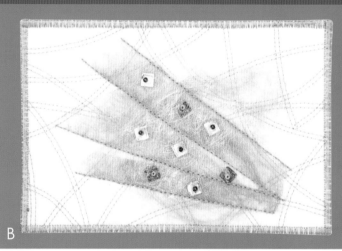

A B

C D

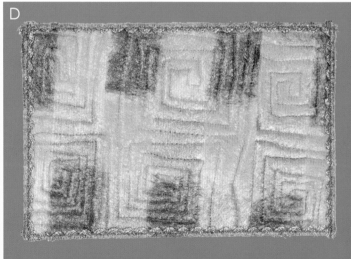

sources

Angelina Fibers

Fusible and Nonfusible Fibers

Button Emporium
914 SW 11th Avenue
Portland, OR 97205
(503) 228-6372
www.buttonemporium.com

Beads and Beading Supplies

TWE/Beads
P.O. Box 55
Hamburg, NJ 07419
(973) 209-1517
Fax: (973) 209-4471
Email: info@twebeads.com
www.twebeads.com

Bubble Jet Set 2000 & Bubble Jet Rinse

Check with your local quilt store
or order by mail:

Dharma Trading Company
P.O. Box 150916
San Rafael, CA 94915
(800) 542-5227
www.dharmatrading.com

Embroidery Designs

**Patchwork Cow, #M1854
Embroidery Library, Inc.**
www.emblibrary.com

Janome America
www.janome.com

Custom digitizing and embroidery designs:

Starbird, Inc.
16305 36th Avenue North, #400
Plymouth, MN 55446-2698
(763) 509-3300
Email: service@starbirdinc.com
www.starbirdinc.com

Fabric and Supplies

Cotton Patch Mail Order
3404 Hall Lane
Dept CTB
Lafayette, CA 94549
800-835-4418 • 925-283-7883
email: quiltusa@yahoo.com
www.quiltusa.com

Sulky Sticky

Check with your local quilt store.

Teflon Pressing Sheet

www.ValerieHearder.com

Threads

www.superiorthreads.com

Watch Findings

The Shoppe att Somerset
22992 Mill Creek, Suite B
Laguna Hills, CA 92653
(949) 380-7318
(800) 877-STAMPER
Fax: (949) 380-9355
www.somersetstudio.com

Vellum Envelopes

Stuffed Ups adhesive envelopes by Sticko, gold #SPSSE10
www.Joann.com

suggested reading

Here are a few of the books and magazine articles that have inspired me to step out of my comfort zone and try something new:

Hearder, Valerie, *Beyond the Horizon*, C&T Publishing.

Hill, Wendy, *On the Surface: Thread Embellishment & Manipulation*, C&T Publishing.

Kolb, Alice, *Sew Crazy with Decorative Threads & Stitches*, American Quilter's Society.

Laury, Jean Ray, *The Photo Transfer Handbook*, C&T Publishing.

Midgelow-Marsden, Alysn, *between the sheets with Angelina: a workbook for fusible fibres*, Evesham.

Newman, Velda, *A Workshop with Velda Newman: Adding Dimension to Your Quilts*, C&T Publishing.

Phillips, Margaret, "Ethereal Angelina," *Quilting Arts Magazine,* summer 2004.

Prato, Cate, "Postcards With an Edge," *Quilting Arts Magazine,* summer 2004.

Warren, Judi, *Fabric Postcards: Landmarks & Landscapes, Monuments & Meadows*, (out of print).

about the author

Franki made her first quilt, a king-size sampler, in 1982. She has been exploring the craft since then on ever-smaller projects. Her current focus on art quilts and experimentation with new techniques and products is satisfied by producing journal pages and fabric postcards.

Franki and her husband, David, live in Oakland, California, where they both enjoy gardening and the companionship of their bichon frise, Mendelssohn.

Photo: Judy Lepire

Great Titles
from C&T PUBLISHING